PEOPLE OF THE BOOK

Yussef El Guindi

BROADWAY PLAY PUBLISHING INC
New York
www.broadwayplaypublishing.com
info@broadwayplaypublishing.com

Cover art by Andrew Skwish

First edition: November 2023
I S B N: 978-0-88145-991-3

Book design: Marie Donovan
Page make-up: Adobe InDesign
Typeface: Palatino

DEDICATION

To John Langs. Thank you for championing this play.
Any new play is a risk, and I appreciated your support
throughout the process.

PEOPLE OF THE BOOK was produced at ACT,
Seattle (John Langs, Artistic Director, Becky Witmer,
Managing Director), opening on September 6th, 2019.
The cast and creative contributors were as follows:

LYNN..Sydney Andrews
AMIR ....Wasim No'mani
JASON..Quinlan Corbett
MADEEHA...Monika Jolly

Director..John Langs
Set design.....................................Shawn Ketchum Johnson
Lighting design..Jessica Trundy
Sound design...Chris Walker
Costume design...Rose Pederson
Production stage manager.........................Jeffrey K Hanson
Production assistant...Kelly McGee
Assistant lighting design...................................Lily McLeod
Dramaturg...Mario Gomez
Dialect coach...Louis Sallan
Fight choreographer.........................Peter Dylan O'Connor
Choreographer...Nadira
Kenan Directing Fellow..Rey Zane

CHARACTERS

LYNN, *early to mid 30s, an artist, European American.*

AMIR, *early to mid 30s, a poet, Middle East American.*

JASON, *early to mid 30s, a writer/ military veteran, European American.*

MADEEHA, *age range can be from mid 20s to mid 30s, translator, Middle Eastern.*

Notes:

1) A slash (/) in a sentence indicates where the overlap starts.

2) The scene shifts should be as fluid as possible.

3) AMIR *will double for the* ARAB MC, *and* MADEEHA *will double for* ZAINAB.

4) The occasional translation of a word is in parenthesis and not to be spoken.

5) The title of JASON's *book (for the prop department) is* Firefight: A Soldier's Memoir.

6) The play runs without an intermission.

AUTHOR'S NOTE

Play this like a mystery. That is, don't play the emotional intensity of later scenes early on. Start light, as if it's a comedy, and stay as light as possible for as long as possible. Things start heating up after Scene 7. However tempted actors may be to hit certain lines hard/harshly, avoid doing so until at least after Scene 7. And even then, don't let the emotions "spike" or get too hot until it's quite obvious things are heating up and, finally, exploding.

Scene 1

(*Outside a bookstore. There's a sandwich board with the name of the store, "Stacked: Books and Cafe", and an announcement for an author reading: "Jason Hanson. Tonight. 7PM."*)

(*A life-size cardboard—or plexiglass—cut-out of a woman with a book in her hand stands next to the entrance. AMIR enters. He wears a coat. He glances at the sandwich board, then focuses on the cut-out.*)

(LYNN *enters from the bookstore.*)

LYNN: What are you doing?

AMIR: This piece of yours: Why is the woman looking up? She's not reading the book.

LYNN: You just noticed this?

AMIR: What is she looking at?

LYNN: She's distracted.

AMIR: By?

LYNN: (*Shrugs*) A handsome guy just walked into the bookstore.

AMIR: Really? You had that in mind when you made it?

LYNN: Sure, why not.

AMIR: So, not really.

LYNN: Why aren't you listening to Jason?

AMIR: I want to know what you were thinking when you made this one? What's the story?

LYNN: The story is you only just noticed.

AMIR: If I was the bookstore who'd commissioned this, wouldn't I want her face buried in the book? You come into the bookstore to buy a book. Not stare off into the distance.

LYNN: And while you're doing that, why not flirt with other book lovers. Come into our bookstore and not only might you find an engaging bedside companion— *(She gesticulates with her hand to suggest the second part.)*

AMIR: You may actually find a bedside companion to go with your bedside companion. Were you really thinking that?

(LYNN puts her arm through AMIR's and hugs him close to keep warm. Perhaps she also plants a quick kiss on his cheek.)

LYNN: Jason saw you leaving.

AMIR: He's still going?

LYNN: He stopped reading when you got up. Didn't you wonder why he'd stopped?

AMIR: I thought it was a dramatic pause.

LYNN: You shouldn't have walked out. He looked upset.

AMIR: He has a big enough audience. One less isn't going to make a difference.

LYNN: We're the only people in there he knows.

AMIR: *You* left.

LYNN: He couldn't see me in the back. You have to be nice to him.

AMIR: I am. But why in particular? I mean I will be.

LYNN: Because. You weren't nice to him before, in school. You have to make up for it now.

AMIR: *You* weren't that friendly either.

LYNN: I barely knew him.

AMIR: Exactly. Which he noticed.

LYNN: How would you know?

AMIR: I have this clear memory in high school, standing close together like this. He's speaking to us, and you're totally ignoring him.

LYNN: I would never have been that rude. I don't remember that at all.

AMIR: What made it worse, your boredom wasn't intentional, you were genuinely bored by him.

LYNN: Really? —Do you think he remembers?

AMIR: Oh he remembers. Guys don't forget things like that. I remember because of the way it made me feel.

LYNN: How?

AMIR: Oh, that I had you and he didn't. —Guys. That age. Here: *(Starts taking off his coat)* You'll freeze.

(As AMIR helps LYNN with the coat:)

AMIR: This is the wrong weather for sexy.

LYNN: A ratty sweater and jeans is not sexy.

AMIR: Dressing up for Jason?

LYNN: That's right, flirting with married men is my thing. You really think he remembers?

AMIR: The girl he had a crush on ignoring him? That's a life-long scar.

LYNN: How do you know he had a crush?

AMIR: I'm pretty sure he masturbated with your breasts in mind.

LYNN: Shut up. How would you even know that?

AMIR: He had that vibe. "Oh God, Lynn Clark's tits, please God let me touch them."

LYNN: Stop.—You think so? No.

AMIR: You're noticing him now. Cleavage in zero degree weather. That's bringing out the big guns.

LYNN: That's exactly what I'm doing. Just for him.

AMIR: Now that he's a famous author.

LYNN: I plan to sleep my way to the top, one famous author at a time.

AMIR: He's a step up from poets.

LYNN: Not my poet. You are an Olympian god among poets.

AMIR: True, true. Now if only poetry had more appeal than something you're forced to endure, like taxes.

LYNN: But who would have thought? Jason Hanson — blowing up like that nationally. He really was kind of a…

AMIR: Nobody?

LYNN: Not nobody. Though you know what they say about nobodies in high school.

AMIR: That only applies to tech nerds and math geeks. *They* grow up to rule the world. Art nerds, not so much.

LYNN: Still. Good for him.

AMIR: Absolutely good for him.

LYNN: *(Looking at him)* What?

AMIR: What?

LYNN: Your tone.

AMIR: What about it?

(The sound of applause from inside. AMIR *and* LYNN *both turn in the direction of the applause for a moment.)*

LYNN: *(About his tone)* Less than enthused. For his success.

AMIR: It's too cold to be enthusiastic about anything.

LYNN: You don't mind his staying with us do you?

AMIR: We can't say no now, not after you invited him.

LYNN: It seemed like the right thing to do.

AMIR: If he doesn't mind the couch.

LYNN: You still want to go out for drinks?

AMIR: Sure. Look, I never disliked Jason. And I am happy for his success. I'm sure after I read the book I'll agree with all this…

(Noticing that the applause hasn't stopped.)

AMIR: …adulation. Wow. They're still clapping. I'm impressed.

*(*JASON *enters.* LYNN *claps enthusiastically. The clapping inside the bookstore dies down.)*

JASON: Hey. I just have a minute. I have to go back and sign books. Are we still on for drinks?

AMIR: I'm sorry I stepped out. The heating in there was too much.

LYNN: I came out to see if he was okay.

JASON: Don't worry about it. Shall I meet you at the bar?

LYNN: We'll wait.

AMIR: Or: We could meet at the bar.

JASON: Let's meet there. This could take a minute. Lots of people lining up. It's around the corner?

LYNN: Yes. Alright. We'll meet there.

AMIR: Congratulations again, buddy. This is really big.

JASON: Can you believe it? Me? It should be you in there. I'll see you in the bar.

(JASON *goes back inside.* LYNN *looks at* AMIR.)

AMIR: Was that …? That wasn't a little dig, was it?

LYNN: *(Rolls her eyes, or some similar gesture)* Don't start. Come on.

(Light change. Transitional sounds or music as AMIR *and* LYNN *step into:)*

Scene 2

(The Bar. Which can consist of just a table and chairs. AMIR *and* LYNN *are seated at the table.* JASON *enters, putting his pen away. Muted bar sounds that eventually fade away.)*

JASON: Sorry. A fan. Wanting an autograph.

AMIR: What can I get you?

JASON: Let me treat you, you're putting me up.

AMIR: Our treat. You're our guest.

JASON: But I can afford it now. I shouldn't be saying this, but—the movie deal might be happening.

LYNN: I heard. That is so great.

JASON: And: a pretty big star wants to play me.

LYNN: Who? Spill.

JASON: I don't want to jinx it.

LYNN: Hints. What movies has he been in?

JASON: Well. He was voted sexiest man last year.

*(*LYNN*'s face lights up and is about to name the actor.)*

JASON: Don't say his name. You'll jinx it.

LYNN: The actor whose name shall not be spoken is *very* cool. *Very* sexy. And he does kind of look like you.

JASON: In a dark room from a distance maybe.

LYNN: Same rugged looks. *(To* AMIR*)* Do you know who we're talking about?

AMIR: Sadly, I do.

LYNN: Doesn't he look like the actor?

*(*AMIR *looks at* JASON. *When* AMIR *doesn't say anything:)*

JASON: Anyway, fingers crossed.

AMIR: So, *Ryan*, what will you have? *(Or substitute the first name of a current movie star.)*

LYNN: *Amir.*

AMIR: I didn't say his last name. You have to say the whole name for the jinx to kick in. What can I get you?

JASON: Anything on tap.

AMIR: *(To* LYNN*)* Usual?

LYNN: Thanks.

*(*AMIR, *noting* LYNN's *enthusiasm, exits.)*

LYNN: What's-his-name really wants to play you?

JASON: So my agent tells me.

LYNN: He does have that hot bod going for him.

JASON: That seems to be the consensus among my female friends.

LYNN: And not so bad yourself. Since I last saw you. You've really buffed up. A lot.

JASON: You think?

LYNN: Yeah, I think.

JASON: Carrying a hundred and forty pounds of extra weight in the field will do that to you. The body has to step up.

(LYNN *reaches out and feels* JASON's *biceps.*)

LYNN: Sorry, I have to feel.

JASON: Please.

LYNN: I've always had a fascination with muscles.

JASON: Off-spring of M4 Carbines. And all the other shit we have to carry.

LYNN: I don't think I've felt biceps this hard. Very impressive. (*She feels them up a little too long. Self-conscious, she stops.*)

JASON: You've filled out nicely yourself.

LYNN: Yup. I got fatter.

JASON: Not that way.

LYNN: Oh. You mean my—? (*Looks down at, or gestures towards her breasts.*)

JASON: No. Well—yeah. Those too.

LYNN: Always had these. I've had cuffs on these babies since puberty.

JASON: I didn't mean that to sound so crude. I actually meant/ in general.

LYNN: Please. I'm guessing the army isn't a finishing school for polite conversation.

JASON: No, it's not.

LYNN: And anyway, I was a nude model for art classes all through college. Being objectified for my body actually has "artistic" connotations for me.

JASON: That's how I look at it, artistically.

(JASON *and* LYNN *look at each other, enjoying the flirt.*)

JASON: Amir looks good. It's great you two are still together. High school sweethearts, marrying.

LYNN: We were too lazy to find other people. Plus we have a few other things in common, like doing art that barely pays. We both seem to be really into poverty. The minimalist approach to stuff.

JASON: I really admired you back then. The cool artists. You had that niche pretty much sewn up.

LYNN: And look at us now. Older with a little extra weight, and a mortgage we can barely afford.

JASON: That's real nice artwork outside the bar.

LYNN: I get a lot of commissions. It's a small town.

JASON: That couple holding hands at the train station: that's you?

LYNN: Yup. Also the painted benches in the park. Big fish in a little pond. You're a big fish in the biggest pond.

JASON: I don't know about that.

LYNN: When you're on all the morning talks shows, I think you can claim big-pond status.

JASON: I'm still trying to get used to all the attention.

LYNN: You deserve it. Going through all you went through. Serving your country. That was a brave thing you did saving that woman.

JASON: What did you think of the actual writing? Apart from the story.

(AMIR *enters carrying the drinks, or maybe it's just a pitcher of beer.*)

LYNN: It's brilliant.

AMIR: What is?

LYNN: His writing.

AMIR: *(Overlapping)* You're talking about the book?

LYNN: He was asking about the actual writing. His prose style. *(To* JASON*)* Right? Amir has/ yet to—

JASON: *(To* AMIR*)* I was wondering what she thought.

AMIR: You're asking about the style?

LYNN: It's great. Straightforward, no fat. Almost like Hemingway. If you're wondering if you're an actual writer, you are. But you don't need me to tell you that. Not when you have the New York Times singing your praises.

JASON: Coming from you, that means a lot. I always respected your opinions.

*(*JASON *turns to* AMIR, *thinking he might add something.)*

LYNN: Amir hasn't read the book yet.

AMIR: I got busy at the gallery right when it came out. But I've read a bunch of reviews outlining the novel and/ it seems—

JASON: It's not a novel.

AMIR: Memoir, and it seems like powerful stuff. No wonder it's being made into a movie.

JASON: You don't have to read it.

LYNN: He wants to.

AMIR: *(Overlapping)* I plan to, tonight.

JASON: Seriously.

AMIR: I want to, really.

JASON: *(To* AMIR*)* Do you remember when I gave you one of my poems to read back in high school?

AMIR: Er…

JASON: Why would you.

AMIR: I think so./ Remind me.

JASON: It was so long ago.

AMIR: What was the gist of it? I'm good with themes.

JASON: Some stupid poem about teenage angst, probably. By the way, congratulations on that poetry prize.

AMIR: Oh. Thank you. Yes. It even came with a little money.

JASON: That's great. How much?

AMIR: *(Taken aback by the question)* I … *(To* LYNN*)* How much was it?

LYNN: It paid a couple of months mortgage.

JASON: Not bad. That's great.

AMIR: We thought so.

JASON: What was the name of the prize again?

AMIR: The Chester Simons Award?

JASON: I don't know that one.

LYNN: So when's the lovely bride arriving?

JASON: Madeeha? Next weekend. The paperwork just went through.

LYNN: That's wonderful. The whole thing. How you met. It's so romantic. Well, not romantic. But—well: it is in a way, isn't it? In spite of the—

JASON: Body count? Yeah. I think so.

LYNN: *(To* AMIR, *quick aside)* You'll know what I mean when you read it.

JASON: Sort of like…never mind. It's a silly analogy.

LYNN: Like what?

JASON: Like that cliche image of the, er—the flower that sticks up through asphalt? You can't quite believe something so pretty could struggle up and survive all those obstacles. So yeah: it is romantic.

(Then:)

AMIR: Sidebar, awkward question. Only because I've never had to deal with this level of attention. How many times have you given that answer in interviews? When asked about her.

LYNN: Did I ask a stupid question?

AMIR: No. I've just always wondered when celebrities get asked the same questions over and over how they cope with that.

JASON: Because the analogy I used is so lame? I did say it was cliched.

AMIR: I don't think it is. I was just feeling bad. I imagine you've had to answer the same questions repeatedly.

LYNN: So you *are* saying it was a stupid thing to ask?

AMIR: *No.* I'm just curious.

JASON: I think my cliche analogy offends his poetic sensibilities.

AMIR: I was wondering how you keep your answers fresh. Or, maybe you've developed pat answers to cope?

JASON: I hope one day you can answer that question for yourself, when some published work of yours is just as successful.

AMIR: *(Slight beat)* Right. —As I said…I've never had to deal with that level of attention. Hence my question.

(Awkward beat)

JASON: And sure, after the umpteenth interview your choice of witty replies does get pretty stale.

AMIR: I'm sure it does. *(Did not mean for that to sound like a further dig)* I mean—. Not that the answer you gave just now was/ stale.

JASON: But then you never thought I was that sharp to begin with.

AMIR: That's not true. Why would you—? I barely even knew you back then.

JASON: That's right, you didn't. I remember.

LYNN: You know what: we all have early starts tomorrow. Why don't we call it a night.

AMIR: Good idea. I can start reading your book. No excuses for putting it off now.

(*Awkward smiles. Lights shift. Transitional sounds or music.*)

Scene 3

(*Living room in* LYNN *and* AMIR's *apartment. Her life-size cut-outs—perhaps four is enough—fill the room. Among the cuts outs: a replica of the woman reading the book, a girl holding balloons, a man walking a dog, and a librarian with a finger to her mouth as if shushing someone.*)

(LYNN *and* AMIR *will soon start spreading sheets and a blanket over the couch to make a bed for* JASON. JASON *looks admiringly at the cut-outs.*)

LYNN: Just remember: you could have had your publisher pay for a decent hotel.

JASON: And miss out being surrounded by your cool art?

LYNN: So when are we going to meet Madeeha?

AMIR: She must be thrilled to marry an American and get the hell out of there.

LYNN: It was nothing that mercenary.

AMIR: I'm sure it wasn't.

LYNN: I get the sense there's real love and respect there.

AMIR: But it still has to be a relief for her from what I read in the reviews. With her whole neighborhood bombed out.

LYNN: I love stories of people from different cultures marrying up. Long after Amir got boring, it was the only thing that kept him interesting for me.

AMIR: I'm so exotic that way.

LYNN: You are. Anyone who prefers hockey to football and frozen pizza to freshly made is exotic to me. You're a complete mystery to me some days.

AMIR: Have you set up an apartment for yourselves?

LYNN: When she's all settled you'll have to invite us over. Not to be pushy or anything.

AMIR: Let's not smother them just yet. She'll need breathing room to adjust.

LYNN: We'll help if you want. Amir still knows a little Arabic.

AMIR: Yeah. "Hello", "goodbye", "shit" and "go fuck yourself".

JASON: Her English is better than mine. She's an English literature major.

AMIR: No kidding.

LYNN: You married another artist, it sounds like. Not always easy I have to warn you.

AMIR: *(To* LYNN*)* It's the best decision you ever made. Apart from the whole—

LYNN: Poverty thing.

JASON: She mostly translates.

AMIR: Do you need anything else? A glass of water?

JASON: I'm good.

(Amir or Lynn will deposit pillows on the couch at some point.)

Lynn: Help yourself to anything in the fridge.

Amir: And I'm going to go start on your book.

Jason: Thank you. For your hospitality.

Lynn: Thank you for your service. I know that's what people say but I do mean it. Or is that too annoying to hear?

Jason: No. I appreciate it.

Lynn: I heard it rubs some vets the wrong way.

Jason: Not me.

Lynn: We get to be artists expressing ourselves freely because of what people like you did.

(Jason looks to Amir.)

Amir: Ditto.

(On impulse, Lynn hugs Jason.)

Lynn: I'm so glad you're home, and safe. And… everything. What an awful experience.

(Jason and Lynn break. A small awkward beat, then feeling the pressure to do it as well, Amir steps in and hugs Jason.)

Amir: Yeah. Welcome home, buddy.

(Amir pats Jason on the back. They break.)

Lynn: Okay. Well…goodnight.

Jason: Goodnight. And thank you again.

Amir: That couch has seen a lot of good times, just so you know.

Lynn: *(Playfully)* Shut up.

Amir: I'm just saying. May the juju of those good times rub off on you, and—so on. Goodnight.

Lynn: Goodnight.

JASON: 'Night.

(LYNN *and* AMIR *exit.* JASON *unbuttons and takes off his shirt while looking around the room and the artwork.* LYNN *renters carrying a blanket, which she deposits on the couch.*)

LYNN: In case you need an extra blanket. Some mornings we wake up feeling like popsicles, even with the heating.

JASON: Thank you.

LYNN: Well…nighty-night.

(LYNN *goes in for another hug.* JASON *and* LYNN *hug. He holds on. Then he kisses her. Surprised, she doesn't resist. It continues for a few seconds before she pushes him away, or takes a few steps back. They keep their voices down when they speak.*)

JASON: Sorry. —Sorry. Shit.

LYNN: It's okay. I…it's okay. Just. Yeah. Goodnight.

JASON: I didn't mean to, uhm—

LYNN: Don't worry about it. I get it. I mean…yeah.

JASON: I'd…I'd like…I would really like to kiss you again.

LYNN: Well…you can't.

JASON: I know, but…do you want to?

LYNN: Jason…you just got married. One of our spouses, mine, is right outside.

JASON: *(Moving closer)* But if none of those things existed—would you want to?

LYNN: They do exist.

JASON: But if they didn't? If we could just do what we wanted.

LYNN: But they do. We can't.

JASON: Lynn. You have no idea how much I've wanted to kiss you. All these years. You've so been in my head. When I was over there it was you. It was you I thought about all the time.

LYNN: Jason.

JASON: I couldn't stop thinking about you, about the way you made me feel back then.

LYNN: You're *married*.

JASON: I really want to kiss you again.

LYNN: Stop.

JASON: Lynn.

LYNN: No. Stop.

JASON: Alright. —Alright. I'm sorry. —I'm sorry. *(Perhaps he shakes his head in disbelief at his actions.)* Goodnight. Please—forgive me.

LYNN: It's okay. It's…yeah. It's past. —Never happened, okay?

(JASON looks at LYNN. They look at each other. She isn't leaving. They kiss. Then she leaves. He stands where he is for a few seconds, a little discombobulated. He sits down on the couch. Perhaps he puts on an undershirt. Then he lies down. Lights transition to:)

Scene 4

(JASON's dreamscape. Perhaps a sound filters in that functions as a backdrop to the other sounds that are heard periodically. Lights up on several of LYNN's life-size cut outs: the girl holding a balloon, the woman reading a book, the man walking a dog, accompanied by barking sounds. There's the sound of balloons popping. Which segues into sounds of shots being fired. He is up by this point reacting to the popping/ gun fire sounds.)

(Perhaps also the sounds of an approaching helicopter and louder gunfire. Also, if possible, roaming spotlights as if shone from the unseen helicopter.)

AMERICAN SOLDIER VOICE 1: Shut that fucking dog up!

(A shot is fired, a dog yelps, the barking stops. Lights up on 4 cut-outs of American soldiers in combat gear spread out on the stage. They are rendered in the same artistic style as the other cut-outs. Jason positions himself between them, crouching down and weaving among them as if dodging bullets. The stage is exploding with different lights.)

AMERICAN SOLDIER VOICE 2: Put your guns by the door where we can see them!

AMERICAN SOLDIER VOICE 3: Break it down! Break the fucking door down!

(Sound of a door being broken down. Then the sound of rapid gunfire coming from all sides.)

AMERICAN SOLDIER VOICE 4: Contact! Contact!

AMERICAN SOLDIER VOICE 1: Haji on the right! Light 'em up!

(Sound of more gunfire)

AMERICAN SOLDIER VOICE 1: Light 'em up!

AMERICAN SOLDIER VOICE 2: Ali Babas from all sides!

AMERICAN SOLDIER VOICE 3: Get the fuck out now! Bug the fuck out of this hole!

(Crackle of military radio and voices of two American soldiers issuing commands. Also, the sounds of continuing gunfire exchanges.)

(JASON has been turning in one direction, then another as he deals with enemy fire. The cut-outs of the soldiers are shot at and fall one by one until only he is left standing. At which point:)

(Lights change. Dream shifts as if JASON *is now in a TV show. Soundscape changes to applause. An* ARAB MC *dressed in a gallebeya and wearing a skullcap comes on holding a microphone. He speaks with an accent.)*

ARAB MC: Congratulations, Private Jason! Last man standing. Give it up for the man!

(More applause.)

ARAB MC: I was really hoping you'd make it to the final round and here you are! My main man! How's it feel?

(The ARAB MC *will position the microphone in front of* JASON *every time he expects an answer.)*

JASON: *(Looking at the fallen cut-outs, horrified:)* Are they all dead?

ARAB MC: God in his wisdom has taken them to a much better place. But you're still in the game, my friend.

JASON: *(Half to himself)* No.

ARAB MC: You are one lucky son of a bitch. Now answer correctly our one and only question and you'll be our winner. Are you ready to be our winner? *(To the audience)* Are we ready to see him win?

AUDIENCE: *(Applause)* Yes!

JASON: What's happening?

ARAB MC: You're on the most popular game show in all of the Middle East: *(He holds the microphone out as if to the audience.)*

AUDIENCE: *Truth Or Die!*

ARAB MC: Here's your question.

JASON: I don't understand what's going on.

ARAB MC: Why did you come all the way to a foreign land and blow shit up? *(To the audience)* Yes! You heard me. We're not afraid to ask the tough questions on this show, people. We say truth or die.

JASON: *What?*

ARAB MC: Would you like me to repeat the question? Why did you come alllll the way to a country that had nothing to do/ with—

JASON: I came to help.

(Sound of a buzzer indicating wrong answer.)

ARAB MC: *(Inhales out of disappointment)* Oooh. Sucks to crash and burn. *(As if hearing something through an earpiece)* Wait. You know: we like you so much we're going to give you another shot to answer correctly.

JASON: I—I did come to help.

(Buzzer)

JASON: I came to be of service.

(Buzzer)

JASON: I wanted to serve my country.

(Buzzer)

ARAB MC: You're killing me. Stop with the obvious.

JASON: I wanted to make a difference and make us safer.

(Buzzer)

JASON: And help build schools, and give women here a chance.

(Buzzer, and boos from the audience.)

JASON: What's with the fucking buzzer!

ARAB MC: The name of the show is *Truth or Die*. I don't make the rules. Our all powerful buzzer is the finest B.S. detector in any unconscious anywhere.

JASON: I came for fucking revenge! Okay?

(The audience gasps in appreciation.)

ARAB MC: I'm not hearing the buzzer. But I'm not hearing the ding-ding-ding either, which means you're *very* close. Keep going, my friend.

JASON: I don't want to play this game. I want to get out.

ARAB MC: We want to give this to you so bad but you have to give us something more, buddy.

JASON: How about this: you blow shit up in my country I'll come and blow shit up in yours.

(Appreciative sounds from the audience.)

ARAB MC: We like the sound of that, keep going.

JASON: You're a backward, camel-fucking tribe of rag heads who should be nuked back into the Stone Age. That's why I came.

(More sounds of appreciation from the audience.)

ARAB MC: This is so great. I love this guy. Don't we love this guy?

(The audience cheers, applauds.)

ARAB MC: One more push for the prize, Jason.

JASON: And… *(He hesitates.)*

ARAB MC: Don't hold back now. You won't believe the prize.

JASON: I wanted the thrill, okay? I wanted to experience something none of my asshole friends back home had so they'd never look down on me again. I wanted bragging rights. I wanted respect!

(The "ding-ding-ding" winning sound is heard.)

ARAB MC: *(To audience)* I don't know about you, but I just came in my gallebeya. Ladies and gentleman, we have a winner!

(ARAB MC *holds up* JASON's *arm like he's won a prize fight. Cheers and applause*)

JASON: Did I win?

ARAB MC: You betcha.

JASON: What did I win?

ARAB MC: Bring out Private Jason's prize.

(*A woman,* ZAINAB, *in full niqab, abaya and gloves enters as the* ARAB MC *continues.*)

ARAB MC: For your brutal honesty and showing courage under withering scrutiny, we want to give you the finest flower of our garden, the most dazzling jewel from our jewel box: Zainab!

(*Cheers and applause*)

JASON: What am I supposed to do with her?

ARAB MC: It's what she can do for you, private. Take it away Zainab!

(*The slow introduction to belly dancing music starts.* ZAINAB *begins to slowly gyrate her hips as the* ARAB MC *drags off the soldier cut-outs and exits.* ZAINAB *removes her gloves, one by one. Then the music kicks in and she yanks her abaya away to reveal a belly dancer's outfit. She belly dances for* JASON. *This goes on for a couple of minutes or so, then:*)

JASON: Stop. I don't want this. Get me out. I want to get out. Get me out. Get me out! Get me out!

(JASON *curls up into a fetal position.* ZAINAB *exits. The music stops. The door opens.* LYNN, *and* AMIR *behind her holding a book, enter.* JASON *jerks awake.*)

LYNN: Jason?

(JASON *just stares at them.*)

LYNN: Are you okay?

(LYNN *and* AMIR *look at the scattered cut-outs. Though it could be just one fallen cut-out.*)

LYNN: What happened?

AMIR: Bad dream, buddy?

JASON: *(Looking at the cut-outs)* Did I wreck anything?

LYNN: Don't worry about it, are you okay?

JASON: I'm—sorry.

AMIR: Not a problem, seriously.

(AMIR *starts picking up the cut out[s].* JASON *helps.*)

AMIR: As long as you're okay.

LYNN: *(To* JASON*)* Leave them. *(Or "it" if it's just one fallen cut-out.)* We'll take care of it.

JASON: Shit.

LYNN: Nothing's damaged. It's all surplus anyway.

AMIR: We've got it.

JASON: I don't know what happened.

(JASON *then hurriedly dresses/ puts on his shoes.*)

AMIR: I used to sleep walk myself. One time I almost flipped my mattress out the window.

LYNN: Good thing I wasn't married to you then.

AMIR: You would have been airborne for sure.

(LYNN, *noting how distressed* JASON *still looks:*)

LYNN: It's no big deal, Jason. Why don't we make some coffee.

AMIR: I'll go start a pot.

JASON: I've got to/ go.

LYNN: Or something stronger. I wouldn't mind bourbon.

AMIR: Great idea. Three shots coming up.

JASON: I appreciate it but I really have to go.

LYNN: It's still dark. Go in the morning.

AMIR: *(Looking at his watch)* You still have three hours before your train.

LYNN: Please don't be embarrassed if that's/ why you're—.

JASON: *(Starting to exit)* I'll call you.

LYNN: Can't we at least have a quick coffee?

JASON: I'll call you. *(He exits.)*

LYNN: *(Calling after him)* Jason… Should we go after him?

AMIR: I think he wants to be alone.

LYNN: He'll freeze out there. Even in the station he'll freeze.

AMIR: He grew up in Alaska, didn't he? This is like summer weather for him.

(LYNN looks at AMIR.)

AMIR: Was I supposed to tackle him to the ground? —I guess PTSD is a thing.

LYNN: That was dripping with compassion.

AMIR: What do you want me to say?

LYNN: We're so privileged. We really are. We have no idea what he's been through.

(AMIR rolls his eyes.)

LYNN: Did you just roll your eyes?

AMIR: Please don't sentimentalize him. Even he would gag at that.

LYNN: You're reading his book, aren't you? He's owed *some* compassion.

AMIR: I agree. Yes. Not because of the book, but—yeah.

LYNN: You don't like it?

(When AMIR *doesn't answer:)*

LYNN: You don't?

AMIR: I'm holding off judging until I finish it.

(From LYNN's *look:)*

AMIR: I'm not saying it's bad, I don't know yet.

LYNN: "Bad"?

AMIR: I'm *not* saying that. I need to finish it first.

LYNN: So far. What do you think?

AMIR: So far? *(Shrugs)* It's good.

LYNN: And?

AMIR: It's—good.

LYNN: First impressions.

AMIR: Can I finish the damn thing?

LYNN: You're never been shy about passing judgement after the first pages of anything.

AMIR: *(Hesitates, then:)* Okay, well…I pretty much think it's—I'm getting a distinct whiff of… *(He can't think of a way to be diplomatic.)*

LYNN: Just say it, say what you think.

AMIR: I think it's kind of on the—questionable side of—believable and—not so believable—divide of things. Frankly. *So far.* But I'm only half way through.

*(*LYNN *wasn't expecting this.)*

AMIR: It may have the ring of truth by the end. But that's my honest, first impression.

LYNN: Questionable?

AMIR: A little bit. Yeah. There's something—I don't know—paint-by-numbers about it. From the descriptions of the country, to—

LYNN: "Paint-by-numbers"? What does that mean?

AMIR: I don't know, the whole—ramp up to the fire fight. The way it went down. All so…Hollywood style. Like he's actually writing a movie. And the romance that followed. The way they hooked up.

LYNN: "Hooked up"? They didn't hook up. You can't call the hell they went/ through "hooking up".

AMIR: You know what I mean. Their coming together. Their ending up together.

LYNN: And you would know how they feel because you've experienced something similar? *(Gets her clothes and starts dressing.)*

AMIR: Oh please. We've talked about this. How claiming any experience that ends a discussion usually needs to be examined even more.

LYNN: This is hardly an academic chat. This isn't a debate about point-of-view.

AMIR: Then you shouldn't have asked what I thought.

(From LYNN's expression:)

AMIR: And what's *that* look supposed to mean?

(LYNN shakes her head.)

AMIR: What?

LYNN: I think you're jealous. I actually think you're jealous.

AMIR: I knew you'd think that. That's why I didn't want to say anything.

LYNN: He became more successful. That has to irritate a little.

AMIR: That's exactly why I'm reacting this way, I'm that shallow.

LYNN: Human nature. I get it.

AMIR: Please.

LYNN: And you never supported the war.

AMIR: What does *that* have to do with anything? Nor did you.

LYNN: I supported the troops.

AMIR: So did I. For the most part.

LYNN: No you didn't.

AMIR: I had issues with the disconnect people have between opposing war and supporting the troops *who make war possible.* I think we're allowed a little nuance in our opinions.

(Seeing LYNN *put on her coat.)*

AMIR: Where are you going?

LYNN: I'm going to see if he's okay.

AMIR: Maybe he wants to be alone.

LYNN: *(As she's leaving)* I can give him a ride to the station and wait with him.

AMIR: I'll come with you.

LYNN: I'll take care of it. *(She exits.)*

AMIR: *(Shouting after her)* I'm sorry I don't like the book! It's not a crime.

(Blackout)

Scene 5

(Airport sounds. MADEEHA *enters trailing a couple of suitcases on wheels. She wears a coat and a hijab.* JASON *enters. They look at each other. He comes up to her.)*

JASON: Welcome. Welcome to the States. Let me…

(JASON *takes the suitcases from* MADEEHA. *There are several flashes, and accompanying sounds, as if from cameras. He waves at the cameras. She is momentarily startled by them. She has a slight accent.*)

MADEEHA: What is this?

JASON: Publicity. The publishing house wants to use your arrival to er—post on its website, instagram, etcetera. (*Substitute other social media platforms if need be.*)

MADEEHA: Oh. I see. Yes.

JASON: Try and sell more copies while it's still hot. The attention won't last, don't worry.

MADEEHA: I don't mind. I don't have to hide anymore. "I have burnt my bridges", as they say. I can do interviews if you want.

(*More periodic flashes from cameras.* MADEEHA *waves very shyly to the cameras.*)

JASON: You don't have to.

MADEEHA: I am happy to.

JASON: I doubt you'll need to.

MADEEHA: More interest will come when it is made into a movie, no?

JASON: You heard about that?

MADEEHA: Is it true this famous actor will play you?

JASON: Maybe.

MADEEHA: I wonder who will play me? —I have a good feeling about all this. It will lead to good things.

JASON: Let's see if it happens first.

MADEEHA: "Inshallah".

JASON: Yeah, that too.

MADEEHA: It will be good for you if I am seen by your side? Good for the book? Jason?

JASON: What?

MADEEHA: Wouldn't it look better if you kissed me?

(JASON *looks at* MADEEHA. *A slight beat. He kisses her lightly on the cheek. More camera flashes. He puts his arm around her. The airport sounds fade out. Transitional music as the lights shift to:*)

Scene 6

(JASON's *apartment. He takes* MADEEHA's *suitcases and puts them in a corner. The apartment is small. Bedroom, kitchen and living room are all packed in one narrow space. An overhead light flickers for a beat, before stabilizing. She looks up at the flickering light bulb. [Note to actors: especially in this scene, in spite of some of the occasionally harsh things said, what barbs there are should be embedded in either believable politeness, or thrown away in an offhanded manner.]*)

JASON: It's a rat hole, I know. We'll find a better place. I haven't had time to look for a new apartment.

MADEEHA: You...can afford a bigger home, yes?

JASON: Yes, but, just because the book's selling doesn't mean I'm overflowing with cash. The advance wasn't that big, and—FYI: I know people outside think every American must be rich, but poor people live in America too.

MADEEHA: I know. —But you are not poor.

JASON: Until recently, yeah, I was. It takes a second to remember I can buy stuff now.

MADEEHA: I'm sorry. I was only wondering where I might sleep.

JASON: I'll sleep on the floor. And don't worry, I won't...jump you or anything.

MADEEHA: "Jump"?

JASON: Make a move on you.

MADEEHA: Expand on this "jump" expression, please.

JASON: "Jump your bones"? It means...

MADEEHA: Ah. Yes. So many ways to talk about sex. None of them very pleasant.

JASON: Not always. It's not always crude. Sex isn't a dirty thing, necessarily.

MADEEHA: I didn't say it was.

JASON: Most people find it fun. And healthy.

(MADEEHA *starts taking off her headscarf.*)

MADEEHA: I do not disagree. I am sure we will find fun in it too.

(JASON *stares at* MADEEHA'*s hair for the first time.*)

JASON: Huh.

MADEEHA: What is it?

JASON: I didn't know that head covering came off.

MADEEHA: *(Amused)* Silly. *(She arranges her hair to be more presentable.)* We are married now. I don't have to hide anything anymore. This is okay? This style?

JASON: It's fine.

MADEEHA: I can change it if you like.

JASON: Whatever suits you.

MADEEHA: I can grow it longer. *(If the actor has long hair, she can say "I can cut it shorter.")*

JASON: I really don't care. *(Correcting himself in case it came across as dismissive)* It's nice. I like it. *(He does genuinely like this look.)* It's nice.

MADEEHA: Good… Where do I hang my clothes? In there? *(She points to an off-stage area. Then goes to open a suitcase.)*

JASON: Anywhere. You can take what space there is. My stuff is in storage, most of it.

MADEEHA: Oh: I have brought you something.

(MADEEHA takes out a tin box and hands it to JASON.)

MADEEHA: You liked this, I remember.

(JASON starts opening it.)

MADEEHA: I wasn't sure if customs allowed cooked food. I would have been sad if they took it.

JASON: *(Seeing the contents)* Is it that baklava thing?

MADEEHA: Yes. Try one.

(JASON takes the box and selects a piece. He is about to bite into it when he hesitates, and holds out the baklava to MADEEHA.)

MADEEHA: They're for you.

JASON: Ladies first.

MADEEHA: *(A laugh)* They're not poisoned, if this is what you're worried about.

JASON: Just trying to remember my manners.

MADEEHA: *(Takes a small bite)* See? *(Making fun of the moment)* Safe.

(JASON eats one.)

JASON: They're good.

MADEEHA: You can have as many as you want now. Lucky you married the chef.

(JASON goes and pours himself a drink.)

MADEEHA: Can I have a drink too?

JASON: It's alcoholic.

MADEEHA: I don't mind.

JASON: I thought it was forbidden.

MADEEHA: Are you my imam now?

JASON: A little hypocritical isn't it?

MADEEHA: It's not a big deal. Muslims drink.

JASON: *(Under his breath, in a jokey, ironic manner)* Muslims do a lot of bad shit.

MADEEHA: Some traditions even say it has some health benefits. The religion does advise against it because bad things can happen under its influence.

(JASON pours MADEEHA a drink. He will pour himself a couple more as the scene progresses.)

MADEEHA: And I would point out that humans in general do a lot of bad shit. I share this in common with other people.

(JASON hands MADEEHA a drink.)

JASON: *(Again, in an off-handed, non-aggressive manner)* I wouldn't sell yourself short. You're pretty much in a league of your own.

MADEEHA: What is the meaning of "league" in this context? I know it means "group", "affiliation", but how do you mean it?

JASON: *(Observational, non-aggressive)* It means—you're a piece of work.

MADEEHA: I don't know this expression either.

JASON: *(Observational, non-aggressive)* It means I have to watch my back, hon.

MADEEHA: *(Staying genuinely polite)* "I got your back" is also an English expression I learnt. If I recall I had your back when you needed it most.

JASON: *(Not unkind, whatever he may actually feel)* We're even then. I got you out. *(Toasting with the drink)* Welcome to America.

MADEEHA: All these sayings about our backs. You would think no one trusts each other.

JASON: That's funny. I'm only beginning to get your wicked sense of humor. Did anyone ever tell you you're funny?

MADEEHA: My ex-husband did not have a sense of humor. So no, I received no feedback on this. Thank you for thinking I'm funny.

JASON: Well, you certainly have a wicked sense of something.

MADEEHA: *(Sensing she needs to change the mood)* Jason. I would like to say again, and repeat many times, and publicly when I have the chance: thank you. You saved me from a horrible life. I will never stop being grateful. I hope one day you will see me as more than something that happened to you, and more as a partner who can make your life better. I am very old fashioned in my ideas of marriage. I will be a good wife. We don't have to think of children now, but perhaps in the future we can—

JASON: *(Interrupting)* Children?

MADEEHA: When we are ready. The women in my family are very fond of giving birth. It is like a competition among us.

JASON: Who said anything about kids?

MADEEHA: We can afford to give them a life with your success.

JASON: Back up a second. First of all—

MADEEHA: They will have advantages my nieces and nephews could never dream of.

JASON: First of all, stop talking like I'm a millionaire.

MADEEHA: I understand. But you do have *some* money to raise a family. And you're famous.

JASON: It's a book. Nobody gets that excited about books.

MADEEHA: They are buying many copies. You're in the newspapers and TV. You're not just a soldier anymore, you're a hero. People are celebrating you.

JASON: Okay, about kids? Small detail: people have to make out first before they can have any. Wouldn't we have to get naked and expose ourselves and, you know, make the beast with two backs?

MADEEHA: Surprisingly this expression I know. When you are a literature major, the arcane is your neck of the woods.

JASON: Wait…you are fucking with me. I never quite get when you're dead-panning it with me.

MADEEHA: "Dead-panning"?

JASON: Or was that like a threat? Bringing up kids? Like you're going to make sure we'll be stuck together forever.

MADEEHA: I do not understand what you're saying.

(Again, throughout this, JASON *is not "spiking" in terms of aggression. He is putting a polite lid on whatever he may be actually feeling. As is* MADEEHA, *whose pleasantness and politeness is more genuine.)*

JASON: Whatever money I might've made doesn't change the arrangement. Don't start talking about kids like we're going to walk off into the sunset.

MADEEHA: My father and mother did not know each other when they married. They were almost strangers, but they had a happy marriage.

JASON: This isn't going to be a happy anything. We will wait a respectable time and then go our separate ways.

MADEEHA: We can't do that until the movie is made. And perhaps a year or so after that. The story will feel less authentic if we divorce now. And I am sure book sales will improve even more after the movie comes out.

JASON: You've—really thought this through.

MADEEHA: You have not?

JASON: Why isn't that a surprise?

MADEEHA: You have not thought about it?

JASON: *(Again, not aggressively)* I think I'll take my sanity over a big bank account any day. I may've lost a few marbles in your country but I'm really fond of the ones I still have. And cohabitation with you into the distant future? Don't take this personally, but…maybe not so healthy.

MADEEHA: Jason. *(Breath, calmly)* If I survived what I did—then I think you have no business worrying about your peace of mind. To put you in the picture of *my* mental health, which you have a right to know as my husband: Every day feels like my skull might break open and I will lose my mind. Just when I think I can see what normal life might feel like there is that memory, we share, and many others that appear and make me feel like I might go mad. Neither you, nor I, have the luxury to lose it. And yes, we will sleep together. Why shouldn't you be allowed to sleep with your wife. We might even sleep together tonight. Would you like that? I am not unattractive without my clothes. I was not a disappointment in bed to my late husband. *(She goes to her suitcase.)* The things that made my last marriage not work were—unique. My husband was a monster. You are not. Whatever you think of me,

you are a hero to me. You kept your promise. That is
the mark of a real man. I know I was shy with you in
the beginning. But we are married now. *(She holds up a
red or pink negligee. It is a little gaudy.)* Please excuse me
if you think this vulgar. We have not discussed your
tastes. Perhaps you prefer something more modest. My
choices on the black market were limited. I think this
is more a smuggler's idea of what is sexy. I understand
its appeal to men of course.

(JASON looks at MADEEHA.)

MADEEHA: What? ...Have I offended you in some way?

JASON: You *do* think I am like your ex.

MADEEHA: Why would you say that? No.

JASON: You think I'm some animal and all I want to do
is bone you?

MADEEHA: "Bone you"? This means "fuck", yes?

JASON: *(Again, not aggressively)* I don't want to fuck you.

MADEEHA: I am asking about the expression, not/ if—

JASON: I don't want to fuck you!

*(This stops MADEEHA. She puts the negligee back in the
suitcase. Beat. JASON regrets how he may have sounded.)*

JASON: You do understand this isn't easy for me, right?
...It feels damn near impossible sometimes. You're
the one who's been living an unbelievably hellish life
and think it's just—normal. Before all this I was your
basic...I had your basic dull American life. And it's
kind of gone now, and I want it back.

MADEEHA: I'm sorry.

JASON: Don't...don't keep apologizing for everything.
I'm not looking for—I don't know if you're playing me
with your apologies, or you're pretending to show me
like your—"obedience"? We don't do that shit here.

MADEEHA: People don't apologize in America?

JASON: Wives don't have to obey their husbands.

MADEEHA: Nobody says "sorry" to each other? Or is this just in New York?

JASON: I'm saying you don't…never mind. We don't have to sleep with each other. That's what I'm saying.

MADEEHA: You don't desire me?…You have not thought about it?

JASON: Of course I've thought about it.

MADEEHA: And? …Is it a pleasurable thought? When you think about it?

JASON: *(Slight beat)* Mostly. Yeah.

MADEEHA: Why only "mostly"?

JASON: You know the answer to that.

MADEEHA: Because of how we met?—Jason: I did and said what I had to to survive. But we both want the same thing. I want an ordinary life just like you. I think we have earned this. I would also like to be—attractive to you. I would like you to want me as a wife. If you wish to divorce me eventually, so be it. But we are together now.

JASON: *(Slight beat)* What about you? I never felt you were attracted to me—ever. You were like get-the-hell-away-from-me.

MADEEHA: This is not accurate.

JASON: Even repulsed.

MADEEHA: I was scared. I didn't know who you were, or what would happen. But I am not scared anymore.

(Beat)

JASON: Yeah. Yeah, I would like to sleep with you.— Yes.

MADEEHA: Good. This will help. Being married to someone you find unattractive would be difficult.

JASON: Do you want *me*, physically?

MADEEHA: I would prefer that you like me first. And not hold anything against me.

JASON: Same here. I have zero interest in forcing myself on you. If you want to go to bed with me, then—I'll probably feel the same way.

(Slight beat.)

MADEEHA: You can…kiss me again. More intimately than you did at the airport—if you want. I would like that.

(Beat. JASON *and* MADEEHA *both feel awkward. Then, remembering:)*

JASON: Oh. Yeah. I forgot. A couple of my friends are coming over for dinner next week. They want to meet you. I already mentioned one of them to you. The poet guy? Amir?

MADEEHA: Amir Morsi?

JASON: His wife is also an artist.

MADEEHA: That will be lovely. I was able to find some of his poems online. He is a very good poet. I translated some of his poems into Arabic just for fun. I'll cook something special.

JASON: There's no room to cook here. We'll order in.

MADEEHA: As you wish. Can we order those Chinese foods in those takeaway boxes I see on television?

JASON: Sure.

MADEEHA: I can pretend I am one of those fun characters on American TV shows. Thank you for introducing me to your friends.

(JASON *and* MADEEHA *end up close together now. They lean in, kiss. They break.*)

MADEEHA: How was that? —I was not sure if I should introduce my tongue. Next time, yes? That would show more intimacy…

(*Slight beat. Blackout. Transitional sound or music as the next scene is quickly set up.*)

Scene 7

(JASON's *apartment.* MADEEHA—*wearing her hijab again*—JASON, LYNN *and* AMIR *are sitting or standing.* MADEEHA *eats out of a Chinese take-out box. The others eat on plates.* MADEEHA *is having a hard time with her chop sticks. The cut-out of the librarian, a present from* LYNN, *is seen.*)

MADEEHA: I am very clumsy with these chop sticks.

JASON: Use a fork.

MADEEHA: I want to do it like I see on TV.

LYNN: (*Trying to make* MADEEHA *comfortable*) I wouldn't mind switching. (*She gets herself a fork, and picks one up for* MADEEHA *too.*) My fingers get twitchy after a day working on a project.

MADEEHA: I am sorry for eating out of a box. It is perhaps rude in real life.

LYNN: It's whatever-you-want-to-do.

(MADEEHA, *taking the fork offered:*)

MADEEHA: I don't think they eat out of boxes in China.

AMIR: They don't have fortune cookies either.

MADEEHA: That's what I like about this country. They take something from another country and make it fun.

AMIR: That's one way to look at it.

JASON: It's a proud tradition. It's called innovation.

AMIR: That's another way to look at it, yeah.

JASON: You have a problem with innovation?

AMIR: I don't get hung up on what others might call appropriation. But, for others, that's—that's what it is.

JASON: What's being appropriated exactly?

LYNN: You were saying about your ex-husband?

JASON: There's nothing wrong with changing something to your liking.

AMIR: Yes, true. But—. There may be some kind of, I don't know—cultural copyright involved? Ethically speaking? Like it's not really yours to change? But—on the other hand, you're right, why not.

JASON: It was Chinese immigrants who changed it for their new customers.

AMIR: I'm with you, sure.

JASON: Everyone adapts. It's called survival.

AMIR: Though some would bring up the whole thing about authenticity. Like what you're eating is not really Chinese food.

JASON: If the Chinese in a Chinese restaurant are cooking food and calling it Chinese, I think we can pretty much say it's Chinese.

AMIR: For American taste buds. I think the Chinese who visit the country may not recognize it.

LYNN: Can we move on from this fascinating topic?

JASON: Then it's American Chinese. But it's still Chinese. It's not Italian.

MADEEHA: I love Italian.

AMIR: But maybe adulterated? I think that's the point. It's not the real thing.

JASON: That's nitpicking. And stupid.

AMIR: I'm just saying what some people think.

JASON: Okay, so what do *you* think?

AMIR: Oh I don't care either way, I just eat it.

JASON: Then why did you bring it up if you don't care?

AMIR: Did I bring it up?

LYNN: Are we done?

MADEEHA: I did not mean to cause an argument, I'm sorry.

LYNN: You didn't. It's one of those silly American non-issues that don't actually mean anything.

JASON: Yes it does. It means this is what makes us unique. We welcome other people's traditions, all kinds, but we tweak them.

AMIR: I'm with you.

JASON: It didn't sound like it.

AMIR: I'm giving another point-of-view. Which is another proud tradition: debate. And one argument says that by making other people's originality "less foreign", we are robbing them of their essential difference. We are Americanizing them out of their original taste. We're dumbing it down.

LYNN: Oh my God. Can we just enjoy the fucking food and talk about something else?

AMIR: Sure.

(*Slight beat as they eat.*)

AMIR: I like this restaurant. We should remember the name next time we're in town.

LYNN: Madeeha: how are you doing?

(JASON *gets up and pours himself a drink.*)

MADEEHA: I am very happy.

JASON: Anyone want a drink?

AMIR: Soda's fine.

LYNN: No thanks.

JASON: Honey?

(MADEEHA *doesn't realize* JASON's *talking to her*)

JASON: Madeeha?

MADEEHA: No thank you. I should be doing that.

JASON: *(To* MADEEHA*)* Relax.

LYNN: You were saying something about your ex-husband earlier?

MADEEHA: Oh.—I was just agreeing with Jason's point. He was not a good man. To put it politely. But I do not wish to talk of an unpleasant subject when we are having fun.

LYNN: I think we can dial down the fun we were having. Unless it's uncomfortable to talk about. Of course it is, never mind. Amir shouldn't have brought up the subject.

AMIR: *(Defensive)* I was—curious. After reading the book.

MADEEHA: It's okay. I don't mind talking about my ex. He is safely in the past. My late husband was a monster and Jason saved me from that life. That is the whole story. With a few details in the middle.

LYNN: That's the problem with reading anything, even non-fiction. You take it in as just words. You know it's true, or based on real events, but at the same time it's in a book, several times removed. The actual horror lived through is somehow—well, papered over. Because it's now been turned into a story. Does that make sense?

MADEEHA: I understand. But there is a happy ending. I'm safe. "Alhamdulillah"*(Thank God)*.

LYNN: Thank God, yes.

AMIR: *(Overlapping)* "Alhamdulillah".

LYNN: It's terrible you had to go through it in the first place.

MADEEHA: We learn from telling these stories. As Jason has so eloquently done.

AMIR: He does sound like a piece of work your ex. That section where Jason quotes you as saying that he liked to pour/ hot water—?

LYNN: *(Warning:)* Amir?

AMIR: It's in the book. It's public, right?

LYNN: *(To* MADEEHA*)* I'm assuming you okayed everything that went into the book?

JASON: Why wouldn't she. She comes out great.

MADEEHA: Jason convinced me my story might help other women.

AMIR: That's the spirit in which I was asking.

LYNN: I'm not sure asking about someone else's pain is dinner conversation. My fault for encouraging it.

MADEEHA: *(To* AMIR*)* Please. What is it you want to know? There is a point you want to make, I think.

AMIR: No. I was just—I was wondering if your husband—Tarek, was it?

*(*MADEEHA *nods.)*

AMIR: If Tarek was… Because he comes across as such a horrible man. And I have no doubt he was. But—I do wonder—without in any way questioning or diminishing the awfulness of his actions, I did wonder—

LYNN: *(Warning him off)* Sweetie?

AMIR: *(Overlapping)* if he was— *(To* LYNN*)* What?

LYNN: Let's not?

AMIR: I was just curious since she's— *(To* MADEEHA*)* since you're here and I can ask directly, *only* if you don't mind.—

*(*MADEEHA *smiles, shakes her head.)*

AMIR: If your ex was—was really as over-the-top hideous as Jason described him?

JASON: What are you saying?

AMIR: I have no doubt he was, of course, but I wondered/ how much was—

JASON: You think we made it up?

AMIR: No no. I was just…

*(*AMIR *sees* LYNN *over-pouring herself a glass of wine, almost to the top of the wine glass.)*

AMIR: You know what: Lynn's right. This is not the right time. I'm sorry.

MADEEHA: I think I understand the question. Yes, it is strange even for me, with my education, to realize how a woman, how *I* could live believing I must always be in the wrong. Why else would he keep hitting me? You even begin to believe: if I am being hit, it must mean he cares for me. Only a man who loves you this much would give you this much attention. Imagine. I knew a woman who thought her husband had stopped loving her because he'd stopped hitting her. If love is measured in this way, my husband's affections were never in doubt. And finally my husband loved me so much he used my body as a shield when the Americans came to our house. When Jason's comrades were killed, Jason could have run. But he didn't. When my husband's friends came with guns, Jason would not retreat. He saw I needed help. He was outnumbered but he managed to remove me from harm. I am sorry my ex was killed in this way, but if I am honest, I am only a little sorry. There is such a thing as evil, Mr. Amir.

AMIR: Just Amir.

MADEEHA: My part in this wrong: I didn't try harder to escape. However impossible escape was in my country. For someone in my situation. That is the story.

LYNN: *(Squeezes* MADEEHA's *hand if she's nearby)* You are not responsible in *any* way. Not even a little bit.

MADEEHA: Jason came to see me in the American compound. I was put there because my neighbors now saw me as a collaborator. Jason and I came to grow fond of each other after many visits. *(Visibly upset)* I always think I will speak of this without emotion, and then I am surprised when I get upset. I am sorry. I will be right back. *(She heads for the bathroom but turns to say:)* I didn't mean to cause an argument about the food.

AMIR: You didn't.

LYNN: Trust me, you didn't.

(MADEEHA *starts to go into the bathroom.*)

LYNN: *(To* MADEEHA*)* Would you like me to go with you?

MADEEHA: I think the bathroom is too small for two people. But thank you.

(MADEEHA *exits into the bathroom. They lower their voices when they speak.*)

LYNN: *(Looking at* AMIR*)* Great. We upset her.

AMIR: *(Defensive)* I thought it was okay to talk about the book.

LYNN: It's not just a book is it.

JASON: It's healthy for her to talk. Seriously.

LYNN: It blows me away when I think about it. And hearing it from her—I get it now.

AMIR: Get what?

LYNN: *(To* JASON*)* Why you two bonded. Going through something so horrific together.

AMIR: How does that follow?

LYNN: What do you mean "how does that follow"? Of course it follows. Two people bonding over such trauma.

AMIR: *(Still trying to figure it out)* Okay. Yeah.

JASON: *(To* AMIR*)* You don't believe Madeeha? Or me?

AMIR: No. I didn't say that. I was responding to Lynn's automatic assumption. 'Cause just the opposite could follow, couldn't it? I mean, you would know. But — where—you *wouldn't* want to be anywhere near the person who reminds you of something so horrible?

JASON: I never really got how unpatriotic you were before. *(He opens the freezer of his small fridge.)*

AMIR: *What?*

JASON: I always thought it was just that elitism thing. Too snobbish for something as lowbrow as patriotism. But it's what Lynn said. With your, *(To* LYNN*)* how did you put it? *(Back to* AMIR*)* Your background? You can never really fully get behind this country.

LYNN: *(Startled)* Excuse me? I said no such thing.

JASON: At the train station?

LYNN: I didn't say that. When did I say that?

JASON: *At* the station. You said his Middle Eastern background makes him doubt the basic good intentions of this country.

LYNN: I never said that. First of all I would never have put it that way, that is so crude. The *most* I may have said was his unique background gives him a different—perspective on the wars.

JASON: That's not what I remember you saying. That's way more nuanced than/ what you said.

LYNN: You're remembering it wrong. I absolutely didn't say that.

JASON: You know what: we've run out of ice cream. *(Grabs his jacket, to* AMIR*)* I'd hate for you to think I'm not a good host on top of my other failings.

LYNN: Fuck the ice-cream. Take back what you said.

JASON: But you did say it.

LYNN: I did not. And what are you still doing with that stupid chip on your shoulder?

JASON: What chip? I wasn't aware/ I had one.

LYNN: "Other failings", that's pathetic.

JASON: "Pathetic", well there you go. *(He heads for the door.)*

LYNN: Jason. Come back here.

*(*JASON *exits. To* AMIR*.)*

LYNN: None of that came out of my mouth.

AMIR: I believe you.

LYNN: *(Grabs her coat, heads for the front door)* He's not going to drop that bullshit and walk away.

AMIR: Don't worry about it. He probably made that assumption from some off-handed comment/ you made.

LYNN: I didn't say anything that would *remotely* make him think that.

AMIR: Like my not supporting the troops or something.

LYNN: I didn't even say that. No: *(Starts to exit.)* he doesn't get to spread shit that isn't true. *(She exits.)*

AMIR: Lynn. *(Going to the door)* Don't waste your time.

(MADEEHA comes out of the bathroom. AMIR closes the door.)

MADEEHA: Where did they go?

AMIR: To get ice-cream.

MADEEHA: I don't yet know the shops. I would have made sure we had dessert.

AMIR: You just got here, it's okay. *(Awkward moment, then:)* How does it feel? All of a sudden. A new country. It must be quite the rush.

MADEEHA: You are very lucky to have been brought up here. So many conveniences. And democracy, of course.

AMIR: There's that, yeah.

MADEEHA: All these freedoms.

AMIR: True. Easy to take for granted if you're not careful.

MADEEHA: I could never take freedom for granted. I feel like I have escaped from a hundred prisons. Freedom almost feels like something warm, and wonderful. Like the smell of fresh baked bread.

AMIR: Well, wait a while. When your conversation starts shifting to what you've been binge-watching, or the latest diets, your appreciation of those freedoms starts to, well—it starts to drift a little.

MADEEHA: How is your Arabic?

AMIR: *(In Arabic)* "Sabakh al Khar", "Ma'salama", "netche", "khara".

MADEEHA: *(A laugh)* Good morning, goodbye, fuck, shit.

AMIR: Excuse my French.

MADEEHA: That's very good. I love your poems. I translated two of them.

AMIR: You did?

MADEEHA: *(Goes to find them in her suitcase, or wherever's she's put them)* Jason mentioned you were a poet. I searched for your poems online.

(MADEEHA gives AMIR the poems in a folder. He will open the folder and look them over.)

AMIR: I'm—flattered.

MADEEHA: First I translated them into Arabic, and then, as an exercise, I translated them back into English. Literal translations can be so funny. Arabic is so expressive. Too expressive. "Alf salaama", "a thousand salutations". Why a thousand? A dozen isn't enough? Or to say you lose respect for someone, which literally means, "he fell from my eye".

AMIR: Thank you—for these. I look forward to reading them.

MADEEHA: Your wife was very kind to give me this gift. *(She points to, or goes up to the cut-out.)*

AMIR: Being a translator she thought it might appeal to you. Your English is excellent.

MADEEHA: Knowing English saved my life.

AMIR: You mean you were able to communicate with Jason at a pretty scary moment?

(MADEEHA nods.)

AMIR: You've certainly been through, not an exaggeration to say "hell". Your story, it's…it's certainly a page turner, for sure.

MADEEHA: It is perhaps wrong that people's stories of misfortune become entertainment for others. But this is the way it has always been. Sitting around a camp fire in caves. Someone tells a story of how so-and-so got eaten by a tiger. And how he should have done this or that. So next time people do not get eaten.

AMIR: And yet people still get eaten. Not so much by tigers anymore.

MADEEHA: And so people have learnt.

AMIR: And what are we to learn from Jason's story, and yours? If you don't mind my asking. By the way, if any of this, if something I say upsets you or, if you don't want to talk about it just say so and: the end.

MADEEHA: I don't mind. If my experience helps other women and shows the bravery of Jason, I am happy to talk. I explained to Jason what he had saved me from. Not only in that moment when my husband used me as a shield, but from the many years of being treated badly.

AMIR: He sounds like a walking nightmare.

MADEEHA: It was not just being married to him that was bad. His behavior was seen as normal. By my family. My neighbors. *I* saw it as normal. To be treated like I was less than human. This is the evil of the world I lived in.

AMIR: He was an insurgent? Your ex-husband?

MADEEHA: Tarek didn't include me in his business. I know he hated America. Some people are driven mad by other people's good fortune.

AMIR: He fought the Americans because he was envious?

MADEEHA: This is surprising to you?

AMIR: That's a lot to put at risk over envy.

MADEEHA: Some people can't stand to see others do well. We are not so complicated as we imagine. You, a poet, must understand how we are also driven by very basic desires. Envy, ugly as it is, is not uncommon. *(Touching her necklace)* That is why I wear the evil eye.

AMIR: Did your ex feel this way about America *before* the invasion?

MADEEHA: When you live in a safe place like this country, there is much room for all the different shades of gray you find in the craft you practice. But not in the life and death world I lived in.

AMIR: Just to warn you, America is not that safe.

MADEEHA: I know, you have many guns. But I was living with tanks and car bombs, so yes, this country is safer. As I said, there is such a thing as evil. And there is such a thing as a culture that allows this evil to spread. And it is infectious.

AMIR: Well, you certainly have an audience here for stories of "evil" from that part of the world. They love it here. It makes them feel very…er—

MADEEHA: I sense you are offended by this truth?

AMIR: I wouldn't say that, no.

MADEEHA: You do not think Arabs and Muslims can commit evil?

AMIR: I do. They have. Like anyone else around the world. I just think the word "evil" is kind of useless as a description of anything.

MADEEHA: Yes, I think it is just a word for you, "evil".
You cannot imagine how it can overtake a whole
country. You have not seen it in the flesh as Jason and I
have done.

AMIR: Yeah… You must have been a great help
in writing this book. Filling in details about your
situation.

MADEEHA: *(Sensing trouble)* I spoke with Jason about
my past, yes.

AMIR: Your story is basically the heart of the book.

MADEEHA: I do not need to tell you that even true
stories are not transcripts. It takes a brilliant artist
like Jason to take a real life situation and turn it into
something people want to read. His telling of the story
is what makes it shine.

AMIR: But the balance, as you must know as a
translator, is to stick close to the source material. Not
start—fabricating. Because what people respond to is,
"Wow, did this really happen? I'm blown away." And
if they find out it didn't happen, well, they rightly feel
screwed. And manipulated.

MADEEHA: *(Staying polite, genial)* Jason tells me you and
him were competitors in school?

AMIR: "Competitors"? I wouldn't put it that way.

MADEEHA: He said you always thought you were
better than him. Forgive me for being blunt,/ but.—

AMIR: He said that?

MADEEHA: You are questioning the truth of what he
wrote, are you not?

AMIR: No… A little, maybe. But not because we
were "competitors". That's a little dramatic. No. My
concern is—it does seem—everyone—everyone in the
book does seem to come off like a—as if they've been

assigned a role. There's the hero, the villain—and you. And I've no doubt you experienced what you did, but—it does all seem to fit into a kind of—"formula" is too strong a word, but. After you break it down? I'm not surprised it's being made into a movie. And I'm not—well I am, I guess, I am questioning Jason's credibility a little. Maybe. As respectfully as I can.

MADEEHA: *(Again, staying genial)* Mr Amir: your poetry suggests you are a bigger man than this. The envy of others is always a surprise to me when it comes from the people we admire. I think we confuse the grace and beauty of their work with the artist who produced it. Perhaps I should give my evil eye to Jason to wear.

AMIR: *(Trying to be diplomatic)* Here's the thing. There's no easy way to ask about stuff that honestly raise red flags for me. Without it sounding like an accusation.

MADEEHA: *(Again, genial)* And you alone picked up on these red flags? No one else. The many glowing reviews and accolades.

AMIR: *(Allowing a little irritation to filter in)* When a public is in a frame of mind to see a group of people in a certain way, trust me, they'll gobble up any old garbage that confirms their worst opinions of that group, because feeling morally superior is just too delicious. Now I don't know if after your horrible experiences you just hold a grudge against your country and think that part of the world is irredeemable, or—

MADEEHA: *(Barely audible)* I believe no such thing. I wrote no such thing in the book.

AMIR: *(Overlapping)* maybe you just said it to escape because you know that's what Americans want to hear.

MADEEHA: You are making assumptions about me that are wrong.

AMIR: *(Overlapping)* But it just *really* gets my goat, a lot. I actually find it offensive. And racist, frankly.

*(*MADEEHA *puts on her coat. Finally registering what she'd earlier.)*

AMIR: Wait:—

MADEEHA: Mr Amir: I want to thank you for teaching me something valuable.

AMIR: Did—?

MADEEHA: *(Overlapping)* It is a window into America—

AMIR: Did you just say—?

MADEEHA: *(Overlapping)* —that may have taken me months to understand. You have no more worries in this country than how you are seen.

AMIR: Did you just say "I wrote no such thing in the book"? A second ago? Did I hear that right? What does that—? What does that mean?

*(*MADEEHA *tries to exit, but* AMIR *grabs her arm.)*

AMIR: Hold up. What did you mean "I wrote no such thing"? Did *you* write the book? Is that what you're saying?

MADEEHA: You are hurting my arm.

AMIR: Were you like the ghost writer?

MADEEHA: Please, let me go.

AMIR: Just tell me, did you write/ the book?

MADEEHA: You're hurting me, Mr Amir. Please let me go.

AMIR: *(Lets go of her arm)* I'm sorry. I didn't—

*(*MADEEHA *exits.)*

AMIR: Madeeha. *(He steps half way out the door.)* Madeeha. I'm sorry. But did you write it? Did you write the book? Just—. Hold up!

(AMIR *grabs his coat and exits. Spot on cut-out of librarian with her finger to her lips, perhaps. Light change. Transitional sounds or music to:)*

Scene 8

(Street. JASON *enters carrying cartons of ice-cream in a plastic bag.* LYNN *enters from the opposite end.)*

LYNN: What the hell.

JASON: Hey to you too.

LYNN: Why did you say that?

JASON: I'm sorry I ratted on you.

LYNN: You completely twisted what I meant. And by the way I said it in strict confidence.

JASON: It's no biggie. Your husband's allowed his opinion. I also fought for his right to dump on this country.

LYNN: I never said he was unpatriotic. I never said that.

JASON: It's okay. No one gets arrested for that here.

LYNN: Don't try and break up my marriage. It's not going to work.

JASON: I'm sorry I can't be as cool as you about what happened at the train station.

(LYNN takes a breath. Calmly)

LYNN: "What happened"—was a mistake. It's a worse mistake when I hear you bring it up to attack my husband.

JASON: No mistake. It meant everything to me. I was standing at the edge of something and you pulled me back.

LYNN: And I'm happy it did that. Great. But it's past. Past tense. Then. Now. Pre-meeting your wife, post-meeting your lovely wife. *We all just had dinner together.*

JASON: I still want to be with you.

LYNN: And the clear lesson is I can't trust you.

JASON: The lesson is you're not happy with Amir.

LYNN: Couldn't be happier. I'm exceptionally happy. I know how it looks: a married woman makes out with someone who isn't her husband, it suggests things aren't great at home, but, counterintuitively, it could also mean she feels so strong in her marriage, she feels confident enough to have a harmless fling and then return refreshed to her husband.

JASON: Lynn. We made love.

LYNN: *In a rest room. At a train station.* In a dirty stall above a nasty toilet that belongs in a horror movie, where something lunges out of the toilet and drags you down into its bowels. It wasn't exactly a chocolate and roses moment.

JASON: Why did you make love to me?

LYNN: Because.—I wanted to do something to make you feel better. God, just saying that makes me want to slap myself. You looked awful and I—somewhat assisted by lust, I admit. And all the dumb decisions you make when you can't keep your pants on.

JASON: Are you really still in love with Amir?

LYNN: I wouldn't be with him if I wasn't.

(A moment, then:)

JASON: No.—No, I don't believe you. You don't do that, you don't share those kinds of feelings unless things aren't working out at home.

LYNN: I'm not going to explain my marriage to you. And once again, I return to your lovely wife.

JASON: She's… *(Shakes his head)* she's not lovely. She's many things but "lovely" isn't one of them.

LYNN: You're adjusting. It's normal. You're seeing her in a new environment. It's like—haven't you ever felt awkward when you bump into your supermarket cashier on the street? You've chatted with her for years and suddenly outside of that store you can't think of a thing to say to her.

JASON: No.

LYNN: You've seen Madeeha in short bursts in a foreign country and suddenly here she is, not going away. You're panicking. You're like, "I have a wife, and she's here." All the romantic barriers you faced in war are gone and now it's just, "Gee, I need to buy some ice-cream and toilet paper."

JASON: I don't…I don't love her.

LYNN: A year from now we'll be a merry foursome going out for dinner and a Broadway show. Or to the opening of your movie starring what's-his-name.

JASON: No. No. She's…she's a monster.

LYNN: Who is?

JASON: She isn't what she seems. She's a frightening human being. Her husband wasn't the evil one. She is.

LYNN: Okay…I'm saying this as a friend…you need to see someone. Whatever resources the VA has for vets, please: check them out. There's no shame in therapy. It doesn't make you any less of / a—

JASON: She killed her husband. I didn't kill him. He didn't die in a firefight. She murdered him. She went right up to him with a gun and blew his brains out.

And then used me as cover. "Killed in the course of a house raid." Along with my buddies.

LYNN: She killed your buddies?

JASON: No. We had fucked-up intelligence. We didn't know the whole damn insurgency was holding a village confab. We were going after her husband. But then, what was so heinous about what he was doing? He was fighting back against a foreign army. Fine, take him out, I get it. But…

LYNN: I'm not following.

(Perhaps a quiet soundscape of some sort filters in, against which the muted sounds of three or four gunshots will be heard after he says "…she crept up behind him…")

JASON: I was the only one who survived the firefight. Along with her husband. Tarek was still standing. He had the advantage on me. He could've taken me out. But she crept up behind him, and unloaded her weapon into his face when he turned around. Into his face.

LYNN: *(Trying to reconcile what she read in the book:)* So…

(The soundscape will filter out.)

JASON: And that look she had. I've been around sick individuals, some of them in my unit. But this. The joy on her face. If you'd animated her into a cartoon character in that moment I swear she'd have looked like the Wicked Witch of the East. The way her eyes lit up, like she'd at last got her biggest wish. I know in war people's better natures don't exactly shine. But in that room…she was the scariest thing I'd seen in that god-awful sandpit. I don't remember much of that firefight, but I remember that.

(Slight beat)

LYNN: So…what you described in the book—

JASON: Oh fuck the book.

LYNN: It didn't happen?

JASON: Are you listening to me?

LYNN: I'm trying to understand.

JASON: I don't want to go back to that apartment. I don't want to serve ice-cream like nothing's wrong. We're not going to be a merry foursome. I have to get out.

LYNN: Okay. Wait. I need to catch/ up.—

JASON: I can't sleep, I barely eat. I lie awake at night listening to her breathe. I know she's only pretending to sleep most of the time. We lie there listening to each other pretending to sleep. Do you know how creepy that is?

LYNN: Jason, you are way over sharing.

JASON: I'm telling you I'm terrified of her.

LYNN: Maybe she's terrified of you. Have you thought of that? She's been through her own war. She's in a new country, with a new husband. I can't imagine she has fun associations with the idea of "husband". It's going to take time for both of you.

JASON: Have you heard anything I've said? I'm the good guy here. (Wondering how much more he should share:) I don't even know…I'm not sure I even killed anyone while I was there.

LYNN: (Again, tries to digest the new information) Okay. So. Just to clarify: you're saying…she's the one who saved you in that firefight?

JASON: (Hurrying on to change the subject) Fine, don't leave Amir. But I need to know you're in my corner.

LYNN: I am.

JASON: *(Reaches out to hold her)* Don't close the door on us, please.

LYNN: *(Avoiding his advances)* Jason.

JASON: Not sexually, I mean—lean on you. I need to know there's someone I can talk to.

LYNN: I'm here, of course. But you have to promise me you'll find someone professionally to talk to.

JASON: Okay, but just—hear me when I tell you how much I thought of you. It got me through the worst of times.

LYNN: And I'm flattered.

JASON: Thinking of you saved me from going batshit so many times.

LYNN: I'm—that's—I've no problem being the person you masturbated to, that's wonderful,/ but that doesn't mean—

JASON: *What?* Don't put it like that. That's disgusting.

LYNN: I thought—in high school?

JASON: What? No.

LYNN: You didn't? Never mind.

JASON: Not *that* way. I never thought of you like that. But yes, from high school on you've always been this—ideal for me. What you stood for. The way you always saw the good in everyone. I'd give away everything I have, my book, my success, to have you in my life. Even if it's just to meet for coffee now and again and— *(Getting closer to her)* —talk, like we're doing now. And get away from this fucked up situation.

LYNN: Jason.

JASON: I'm acting pathetic, I know that. "There he goes again: still the loser."

LYNN: Stop it./ I've never thought that.

JASON: But I'm not. I'm not a loser.

LYNN: I never thought you were.

JASON: I just screwed up with this one thing.

LYNN: You're a newly married, successful author overwhelmed by a lot of things all at once.—

(JASON *kisses* LYNN. *For a second, she's thrown by the action but soon pushes him away*)

LYNN: And you need to go home to your wife.

(JASON *tries to kiss* LYNN *again, but she pushes him away.*)

LYNN: Jason, I mean it.

JASON: I love you.

LYNN: Go home before the ice-cream melts.

JASON: Fuck the ice-cream.

(MADEEHA *appears. She was probably there to see the first or second kiss. She sees* JASON *clutching* LYNN, *trying to kiss her again.* LYNN *sees her first.*)

LYNN: Madeeha.

(LYNN *pushes away from* JASON, *as he turns to see Madeeha. They stare at each other. Slight beat*)

LYNN: I…I have to go.

(LYNN *starts to exit. Then stops to say something to* MADEEHA. *Perhaps the soundscape we heard a few pages earlier—minus the gunshots—is heard as* LYNN *momentarily stops by* MADEEHA. LYNN *decides against trying to explain herself and exits.* MADEEHA *turns to* JASON. *Again they stare at each other. Transitional sounds of a train as lights dim on them and go up on:*)

Scene 9

(Train compartment on a commuter train. The two seats are occupied by LYNN *and* AMIR.)

AMIR: I promise you it's not envy. It may seem like that but it's not. And honestly: I do have a problem with this whole "support the troops" thing if you're against wars. I'm not going to apologize for that. I don't get the disconnect people have between being against war, while glorifying the people who wage it: *soldiers*. Not pixels on a screen. Though these days who knows with drones and God knows what else is coming down the pike. But even with that there's still a human being operating a killing machine. And I do have a thing— look, yes, it bugs me when I hear of people who join up because they want an "experience". Or to prove they're tough men. Jesus Christ, flying off to a foreign war to show how butch you are? Which these days means killing brown people not whites. You're not going to be sent off to fight Canadians or Australians. All so you can come back home with war stories and a book? No. Sorry. I'm not saying patriotism doesn't play a part, and I know poor people sometimes don't have a choice, but—and again: I'm *not* out to get him. But I'm honestly questioning how much of that book he wrote. She said that. She said it to my face. "I wrote no such thing in the book." Am I misinterpreting that? I asked point blank if she was the actual author and she never denied it. *And: (Takes out the folder, opens it and gives it to her.)* She handed me this. A translation of a poem of mine. She retranslated it back into English. Why? Why would she do that? So I could take note of the *style*. Her idiosyncratic punctuation and line breaks which bears a really strong resemblance to the style in the book, which we both said was unique. Look at it. She *wants* us to know without saying. That's why she gave it to me.

LYNN: *(Hands the folder back)* How wonderful for you if you're right.

AMIR: Lynn. If someone put their name to an art work of yours, wouldn't that matter to you?

LYNN: You're enjoying this too much.

AMIR: Seriously. Why wouldn't you care anymore about basic things we've all agreed on. Like facts. Even a teeny bit of integrity would be nice.

LYNN: Two people who've been through more hell than either of us/ will probably ever experience in our lifetime—

AMIR: Here we go.

LYNN: —and here you are doing your best impersonation of a hyena.

AMIR: A hyena? You're likening someone searching for the truth to a marauding beast?

LYNN: You're not searching, you're *hunting*. Yes, a hyena's about right.

AMIR: Don't you want to know if a national, worldwide best seller, a *memoir*, a piece of non-fiction might be a big fat lie? If someone discovered Rodin's sculptures were all done by his mistress, wouldn't you want to know that?

LYNN: It would still be a great sculpture either way.

AMIR: Oh bullshit. You'd be howling.

(LYNN shakes her head at AMIR's attitude.)

AMIR: Why are you upset at me? *(Holding up the folder)* I have probable evidence. *Handed to me.*

LYNN: You're competing with him again. It just makes you look small.

AMIR: I never competed with him.

LYNN: And you're not competing with him now, are you. He's moved on from the little league of high school.

(*This stings* AMIR. *He stares at* LYNN. *Transitional sounds of a train stopping. Lights shift, scene change. She gets up and exits into their living room. He follows her.*)

Scene 10

(*Though a little time has passed, there should be no break from the last scene into this one.* LYNN *and* AMIR *take off their coats.*)

AMIR: So let me get this straight: you officially don't care for those pesky fact things now. I don't even want to say "truth", it sounds so pompous. Like we might have to live our lives, you know, ethically. So much better just to jerk each other off and feel good.

LYNN: You're a champion of the truth now are you?

AMIR: Shouldn't we all be? Isn't that like basic moral hygiene? I didn't know it was up for debate.

LYNN: When there's something more important at stake, yes it is.

AMIR: What's more important then deciding on a basic set of guidelines for everyone to follow, so shit doesn't fall apart?

(LYNN *starts to exit into the bedroom.*)

AMIR: Don't walk away.

LYNN: I'm exhausted, I'm going to bed.

AMIR: You can't go to bed in the middle of an argument.

LYNN: When you turn into an asshole, yes I can. That's how I've kept our marriage going for this long.

(Interjecting before he can reply) And you don't know his motivation for joining up. How would you even know?

AMIR: When did it become a good thing to be trained to kill, whatever the motivation.

LYNN: To serve something higher than your selfish self, not kill. That's a noble, good thing.

AMIR: You were at the protests just like me.

LYNN: *Do* you love America?

(AMIR looks gobsmacked.)

AMIR: I can't believe you just asked me that.

LYNN: Honestly, I don't know anymore. I don't remember you ever standing up for the anthem, or showing any kind of respect. It's all cynicism and sneering with you. *(She goes and gets a drink.)*

AMIR: Whoa, where did my wife go? Bring her back.

LYNN: We live such privileged lives, we really do.

AMIR: When did you become all right-wing wacko on me?

LYNN: The minute I take pride in something bigger than myself like my country I become a fascist? We really, *really* don't know what it takes to have the kind of life we enjoy. People like Jason who put on a uniform and do the actual grunt work of making sure other countries/ don't walk all over us.

AMIR: Un-fucking believable. You know what else gets boring? Artists whipping themselves for doing what they do. "I must be an elitist, forgive me for trying to contribute to my culture and making life interesting for other people." No, if you want to be considered a "man" join the army and kill someone.

LYNN: By that standard Jason beat you at your own game. He's added more to this culture, he's touched more hearts and minds with this one book than you ever will with all your poems put together.

AMIR: Wow…okay…new low for you.

LYNN: It's a fact. You being a champion of the truth and all.

AMIR: I am. Which is why I don't think he wrote the book. Or he had more help than he's letting on, and I think people should know that. And Madeeha be given the credit she deserves.

LYNN: *That's* why you want to bring him down? To give Madeeha credit? How very big of you.

AMIR: And because of what happened! Hundreds of thousands, a *million* people by some estimates *dead*! Because of lies! Lies that dragged us into that fucking war and books like his that keep all those fucking lies going!

(LYNN *starts exiting into the bedroom.*)

AMIR: If we all start popping lies like Tic-Tac then we're all screwed! I'm not done.

LYNN: (*Off-stage*) Sleep in the living room.

(*The off-stage bedroom door—if it is off-stage—is heard slamming.*)

AMIR: *You* sleep in the living room!

(AMIR *exits—if the door's off-stage. We hear the rattle of a door knob, and a door being kicked once.*)

AMIR: Lynn. Open the door. Open the fucking door.

LYNN: (*Off-stage*) Sleep on the couch!

AMIR: (*Off-stage*) *You* sleep on the couch!

(AMIR *enters the living room looking pissed. He stands there for a beat. Then goes and gets the bottle of whiskey. He carries the bottle to the couch and sits there for a beat. He takes a swig. Then lies down. Lights dim.*)

Scene 11

(A few hours later. The door bell is heard. Followed by knocking. Amir jerks awake. He goes to the front door and opens it. MADEEHA *is seen holding the cut-out of the librarian. She will stand it up somewhere.)*

AMIR: Madeeha.

MADEEHA: May I come in, please?

AMIR: *(He reflexively checks his watch)* Er—sure.

MADEEHA: *(Entering)* I know it is late.

AMIR: More like early. I'll be getting up in a couple of hours.

MADEEHA: My husband is not far behind me. Could you please close the door? He's coming by car. I took the train.

AMIR: O-kay. *(He closes the door.)*

MADEEHA: Is your wife awake?

*(*LYNN *enters the living room in her pajamas, switching on the lights as she comes in.)*

LYNN: Hey, Madeeha. Is everything alright?

MADEEHA: I wish to return this gift. *(Points to the cut-out)* I do not wish to be reminded of what you have done every time I look at it. I also ask you to please leave Jason and I alone. We have enough to deal with without you interfering. I know in his eyes you represent everything I am not.

LYNN: Madeeha. If you're referring to what you saw, nothing happened.

AMIR: What did she see? *(To* MADEEHA*)* What/ did you see?

LYNN: Jason was drunk. He was stressed out and he tried to—he—

MADEEHA: There was more than trying. The kiss was very intimate.

LYNN: It was *not* intimate, trust me. And I pushed him away.

AMIR: He kissed you?

LYNN: You did see me push him away, right? It may've looked bad but please don't read more into it then the dumb, spontaneous moment it was.

AMIR: You kissed him?

LYNN: He lunged at me. Though I'm not sure even *he* knew what he was doing. It was one of those things that mean *way* less than the way they look, I promise you.

MADEEHA: Was it not you who also had intimacy with him at the train station? When he visited you for the book tour?

AMIR: What?

MADEEHA: Did that also mean nothing? Does sex have no meaning here?

LYNN: He told you that?

MADEEHA: Do you all copulate as easily shaking hands? Or is it just you?

LYNN: Madeeha—

MADEEHA: He wanted me to know just how less desirable I am in his eyes.

(LYNN, *off of* AMIR's *look:*)

LYNN: He's lying.

MADEEHA: You deny it?

LYNN: *Yes.* I'm sorry you're going through this— whatever you two are going through but I promise you nothing happened. At the train station or anywhere else.

AMIR: That's why you were gone for over five hours.

LYNN: Don't you start believing this crap. The train was delayed, I told you.

MADEEHA: The happiness in his eyes when he spoke to me about it.

LYNN: It's a lie. He's using me to get back at you, obviously.

AMIR: Why would he need to get back at her? Because she saw you two kissing?

MADEEHA: *(To* AMIR*)* You know your wife better than me. You will determine the truth.

LYNN: Is that why you came? To stir up shit between me and my husband? I'm sorry things are messed up with Jason but don't come into my house and dump your mess here.

MADEEHA: I came to tell you to leave us alone, that is all. I would like a chance to love him in the way I know I can. Please don't ruin that.

AMIR: *(To* MADEEHA*)* What did he tell you happened at the train station exactly?

LYNN: *Nothing. Drop it.*

MADEEHA: I have said enough.

LYNN: Plenty. And by the way, he also said shit about you, none of which I believe, so maybe you shouldn't be so quick to believe what he says about me, yeah?

(The doorbell rings.)

AMIR: *(To* LYNN*)* That must be your war-hero lover.

LYNN: *(To* MADEEHA*)* He followed you?

AMIR: *(Opens the door)* Jason. How nice of you to drop by at five o'clock in the morning; come in, buddy.

(JASON enters.)

AMIR: We were just talking about you. You have such a fan club here. And this time it has nothing to do with the book. This time the question that came up is:—

LYNN: Amir.

AMIR: Did you in fact fuck my wife at the train station?

LYNN: *(To JASON and MADEEHA)* I don't mean to rush everyone out after you just got here, but it's too early in the morning for bullshit. Why don't we all meet again when everyone is less hysterical.

AMIR: Oh come on, Lynn. This man's faced a lot worse than accusations of adultery. He's gone up against scary Arabs with machine guns. Fessing up to fucking my wife should be a breeze.

JASON: You really can't stand my success, can you. You aren't even pretending anymore.

AMIR: I *might* be envious of a real author who wrote an actual book. Not one who's had more help than he's letting on. And by the way, that would make for a much better movie: a swindler. Putting one over the public. I'd go see *that* movie.

(JASON looks at MADEEHA, then at LYNN.)

AMIR: Oh don't blame Madeeha. I smelt fraud from the beginning. Even "poetic license" can't excuse some of those real convenient plot twists, not when it's supposed to be *"non fiction"*.

JASON: How would you even know what happens in a war with the stupid life you lead?

AMIR: And that's how you shut down all questions about your book. The war and your service, which I sincerely appreciate but fuck off.

JASON: *(To* MADEEHA*)* What did you say to them?

MADEEHA: I didn't. I said nothing.

AMIR: I read her translation of my poem back into English. Stylistically, the similarities with the book, I have to say, buddy, this could be quite the scandal.

JASON: You don't know what you're talking about.

AMIR: I *do* know I'm the author of my own work and not a con man. And now that we've established you have the ethics of a con man, could you please get the fuck out of my house.

*(*JASON *takes off his coat ready to fight.* LYNN *steps forward to intervene.)*

LYNN: Don't! Jason!

JASON: Come on then, show me what you've got.

AMIR: You think I can't take you on?

LYNN: Shut up, both of you! *(To* MADEEHA *and* JASON*)* I think you should leave, *now.*

MADEEHA: We do not wish to see you again either. You will keep away from us, please.

JASON: *(To* AMIR*)* Fucking knew it. Hiding behind your wife. Like all the other Arabs I saw over there.

*(*AMIR *breaks free from, or gets around* LYNN, *and physically engages with* JASON. MADEEHA *soon joins* LYNN *in trying to break them apart.* AMIR *and* JASON*'s tussle will end up on the ground.* JASON, *given his training, will clearly get the upper hand in the fight. Interspersed throughout the physical melee:)*

LYNN: Stop! Stop it! Stop it! Jesus, just stop! fuck. I'll call the cops! I swear I'll/ call them if you don't stop!

*(*LYNN *goes to get the pitcher of water from the drink cart. It could also be a water-filled vase with flowers.)*

MADEEHA: Jason. Jason, please, do not fight like this.

(Interjections from MADEEHA *to stop fighting can continue as* LYNN *returns with the pitcher of water. She pours it over* JASON *and* AMIR. *This does the trick. They stop the fighting and separate.)*

LYNN: Are you kidding me? *Are you kidding me?*

(Everyone takes a breath.)

AMIR: *(To* LYNN *and* JASON*)* This is on you two. *(To* JASON*)* And hey: if you want to get rich off your fraud, go ahead. If they all want to celebrate a returning war hero to feel good, milk it. But don't make up for whatever's missing in your life by taking from mine. Don't you dare come near my wife again.

LYNN: Amir.

MADEEHA: *(To* LYNN*)* I would ask the same.

AMIR: Madeeha. I get that you needed to get out. And maybe helping him paint you as some helpless victim in the book is a small price to pay—

JASON: You are so clueless.

AMIR: *(Overlapping)* —but you just make sure you're not backing yourself into something worse than your old life.

*(*JASON, *to* AMIR, *quieter now as he puts on his coat:)*

JASON: You know what I envy most about you: the exact opposite of what I admired about you back then. The way you/ seemed so cool and plugged in.

AMIR: That grudge you still have, wow.

JASON: Now I just want your blissful ignorance. To go back to when I was just a struggling writer and you two seemed like something special. But I did live through something. It did open my eyes in ways I wish it hadn't, in ways you'll never understand. Because all you've done is lived the kind of useless, selfish life that produces poems about sunlight falling on fucking leaves. Because the world needs more poems about autumn fucking leaves.

AMIR: That's why you'll never be a real writer. You've no clue what could be great about a poem about autumn fucking leaves.

JASON: *(A last plea)* Lynn?

LYNN: I think you should go.

(MADEEHA takes JASON's hand and stares somewhat defiantly at LYNN and AMIR. Then she exits with JASON. AMIR walks over and closes the door. There is a silence, then:)

AMIR: Did you sleep with him? …At the train station? …Or anywhere else?

(Another longish silence. LYNN looks like she might say something, but changes her mind. Finally, she stops trying to consider her options.)

LYNN: No.

(Silence. AMIR walks past her and exits. The bedroom door is heard shutting. Transitional sounds or music begins. LYNN sits down. She picks up the nearby bottle of whiskey. Lights dim on LYNN and AMIR's house. A transitional spotlight remains on LYNN as she takes a swig. Then lights up on JASON's apartment. MADEEHA enters with a pizza box. She puts it down and waits standing. There is a moment where LYNN and MADEEHA seem to look at each other. Then LYNN exits.)

Scene 12

(A few moments pass, then JASON enters.)

MADEEHA: Where were you?

JASON: Out.

MADEEHA: May I ask where?

JASON: Walking.

MADEEHA: That must be nice. Going wherever you please.

JASON: You're free to do what you want too.

MADEEHA: No. I am not. I'm married. I share my life with you now.

JASON: In this country, you're not obliged to—

MADEEHA: *(Irritated:)* Stop speaking of my country like it's a different planet. *(Collects herself. Slight beat)* Don't couples here tell each other where they're going? What they're doing? I have so much to learn from the high standards this country sets. Thank you for this lesson on how much better the men here treat their women. Adultery aside.

JASON: If you want a divorce.

MADEEHA: Oh no. No no. I am beginning to understand in this country no one is loyal to anyone. Where I come from betrayal requires more than one little affair. *(Slight beat. Breath, change)* I bought you a pizza. I can heat it up. I see shows where Americans love cold pizza for breakfast. Is this true?

JASON: *(Shrugs)* Some.

MADEEHA: Do you like it?

JASON: Sure. Whatever.

MADEEHA: So you want to eat it cold?

JASON: *(Not really caring)* Sure.

MADEEHA: *(Puts a slice on a plate for him)* I can cook on this small stove if you like. I have made delicious meals on much smaller. Will you let me try?

JASON: If you want.

MADEEHA: I know we'll be moving into a bigger place. But it would be nice to make this more of a home while we're looking. I can make it cozier. Didn't you notice how comfortable my little corner was on the compound?

(JASON *will take the pizza but not eat it.*)

JASON: Yeah. —It looked good.

MADEEHA: *(Noting his mood)* Jason…don't be depressed. It is not as bad as you think. I know we met in a horrible situation. We didn't—what is it called? "Meet cute". Like in those romance movies. But we can create new memories now, around happier things. We will learn to trust each other.

JASON: "Trust"?

MADEEHA: It will take time, but yes. *(Perhaps she peels away a bit of cheese from the pizza and starts to eat.)*

JASON: You think we'll learn to trust each other?

MADEEHA: I have read that in this country the big thing is all about second chances. "Washing the slate clean", I think it is called.

JASON: There isn't enough water for that.

MADEEHA: Don't be like that. I forgive you too.

JASON: *(He drops the plate. Slight beat)* The problem with your plan, as I see it, is…I—I kinda…I kinda feel a little repulsed by you…I know that's a mean thing to say, and I'm sorry. But you just—trigger a deep…gag reflex. I thought I could do this. I did. I acknowledge and thank you for your help in saving my life. But I said yes to all this under extreme conditions. I made promises in a really fucked up situation.

MADEEHA: But you have the book now. It's all in print. The whole story. I think we must stick to this.

JASON: I don't care about that anymore. I don't even care if people think you had a hand in it. Though let's be clear, you may have typed the manuscript, but I dictated it. Those are my experiences, my life story. You may have written that one chapter where I basically blanked out, and added a few personal details, but that's my blood and guts in there.

MADEEHA: I am not disputing that.

JASON: Don't go handing out translations to hint you had some hand in the whole thing.

MADEEHA: Of course you are the author. And that section *is* only one chapter. Everyone who writes their own story has holes in their memory. I filled some of that in, that's all. And a little editing and polishing.— And a few other things.

JASON: And don't think you can hold that over me, because fuck your blackmail. I don't care anymore. I don't care.

MADEEHA: Yes. You do.

JASON: No I don't.

MADEEHA: Of course you do. Your vanity as an author and "brave" soldier demands nothing less than adulation.

JASON: Fuck you.

MADEEHA: Your world would fall apart if others saw you as I did on that day.

JASON: Let them.

MADEEHA: *Now* you are brave?

JASON: Fuck you!

MADEEHA: I have a solution. *(Picks up a paper bag)* If I disgust you so much, what if I wear this in the house? *(She takes a knife and slashes the bag to make holes for eyes.*

She'll place the bag over her head.) Better than a niqab.
I can draw eyes and a red mouth. I can rouge up the
cheeks. I'll get a prettier bag, of course, from a fashion
designer like Channel. This way we can avoid making
your stomach turn every time you look at your wife.
You are so delicate as it is already. Better?

(JASON moves to the front door but MADEEHA blocks him.)

MADEEHA: I haven't finished showing you. *(She starts
getting out of her dress. She will stand in her underwear.)*
I bet Lynn walks around in her sexy underwear. Will
this make you gag less or more?

JASON: Get out of my way.

MADEEHA: Aren't I sexier now? I can buy sexier bras.
You can even pick them out for me.

JASON: Get out of my way.

MADEEHA: And there are creams to make my skin as
light as Lynn's. Give me a week and I'll be just like her.

JASON: You'll never be like Lynn.

MADEEHA: But I can pretend and so can you. *(She puts
her arms around his neck to kiss him.)* You won't even
have to touch my lips if you kiss me through the bag.

(JASON pushes MADEEHA away:)

JASON: Leave me the fuck alone!

*(MADEEHA stumbles back. She pulls the bag off her head and
throws it down.)*

MADEEHA: Leave you alone? —Leave *you* alone? —You
want *me* to leave *you* alone? *(She laughs.)* Oh that is—
what is the literary term for that? Oh, yes, in translation
I think the English is "go fuck yourself".—You…you
invade, INVADE: my country. You attack: *us*. You
trample over *everything—everything*. You destroy—
rob—countless, hundreds of thousands of families of
their loved ones, husbands, brothers, mothers, aunts,

whole clans, you *kill*. You terrorize a WHOLE nation.
You make us kneel before you and *humiliate* us; you
urinate over our heritage, everything, actual *corpses*
you piss on. You break down my door and bring your
violence into *my* house. And now you want me to leave
you alone? *(Another laugh perhaps)* Oh—my sweet,
sweet husband. You who have the soul of a poet if not
the talent, we took a sacred vow, you and I. We are
together now. I am devoted to you in ways that even
love itself can't compete with. And not only because
I saved you. I did save you. You do remember that,
don't you? We didn't put footnotes in the book to point
out the details, but I SAVED YOUR ASS! *(Perhaps she
slams her hands on the table with those words.)* Cowering
like a *bitch* the way you did. That can't be a complete
blank in your memory. You must have seen how you
looked. Didn't you see your reflection after you peed
yourself? Now that's a metaphor your poet friend
Amir could use. Not Narcissus admiring himself in a
pool of water, but a scared little boy staring at himself
in his own *piss*.

*(JASON picks up a frying pan or some heavy object to hit
MADEEHA with.)*

MADEEHA: If that would give you any kind of
backbone, I would tell you go ahead, crack my skull
open. As your wife, I would gift you that.

*(Beat. JASON drops the object. He goes and collapses
somewhere. Beat. MADEEHA will either put her dress back
on or wrap something around herself.)*

MADEEHA: Jason…I understand you have mixed
feelings about me right now…. But I can't be blamed
for trying to survive, can I? Even now it seems I am still
fighting for my life. For both of ours. Did you not see
how I defended you against Amir? …You were not just

a way to escape. I *do* have affection for you. I know that may be hard to see at the moment. But—we're really at the very beginning of our relationship. We both have to give each other a chance. You have to try, as I do with you. You must try and imagine me separate from the horrible thing that brought us together. *I* can imagine you as a brave man. In spite of everything. You have shown yourself to be so. You *did* rescue me. Here I am. Safe. In America. We saved each other. Won't you extend the same generous imagination you show as a writer to me? Imagining me as a loyal wife, who will do her best to make your life easier? "Turn the page". A lovely saying. Can't we do that for each other?... Please?

(MADEEHA *looks at* JASON, *searching for a reaction.*)

MADEEHA: Is that a yes? *(Slight beat)* You are a much better man than you think you are. My job is to prove to you that you're as brave as the world thinks you are. So you believe it. Because then I think you might start accepting me—and not see me as a reminder of your... very—brief moment of weakness. In spite of what I just said. I of all people should know: you can't be blamed for just trying to survive. God only made us human, not superman. *(Slight beat. She gets the slice of pizza.)* And you know what else? Cold pizza isn't so bad.— Now—tell me: what dishes do you like to eat and I will learn to cook them. I will become the best cook ever. And wife. And mother. You'll see. I will surprise even you. I really think I may be more suited to my new life with you in America than you think.

(MADEEHA *positions the slice in front of* JASON's *mouth to take a bite. He hesitates. Then takes a small bite and chews.*)

MADEEHA: I really do.

(JASON *and* MADEEHA *stare at each other. Hold for three counts.*)

(Blackout)

END OF PLAY

www.ingramcontent.com/pod-product-compliance
Lightning Source LLC
Chambersburg PA
CBHW070023110426
42741CB00034B/2419